Unsolved!

MYSTERIES OF THE ANCIENTS

Kathryn Walker

based on original text by Brian Innes

Crabtree Publishing Company

www.crabtreebooks.com

Crabtree Publishing Company

www.crabtreebooks.com

Author: Kathryn Walker
 based on original text by Brian Innes
Project editor: Kathryn Walker
Picture researcher: Colleen Ruck
Managing editor: Miranda Smith
Art director: Jeni Child
Designer: Rob Norridge
Design manager: David Poole
Editorial director: Lindsey Lowe
Children's publisher: Anne O'Daly
Editor: Molly Aloian
Proofreader: Crystal Sikkens
Crabtree editorial director: Kathy Middleton
Production coordinator: Katherine Berti
Prepress technician: Katherine Berti

Cover: The Sphinx, believed to have been
built by the ancient Egyptians, is located in
front of the Pyramid of Khafre in Giza, Egypt.

Photographs:
Corbis: Ron Watts: front cover
Getty Images: Guy Marks: p. 10–11; Jochen Schlenker: p. 21
Istockphoto: Carsten Brandt: p. 7; Hulton Archive:
 p. 6; Ranplett: p. 26; Daniel Wiedemann: p. 15
Kon-Tiki Museum, Oslo, Norway (www.kon-tiki.no): p. 9
Museo del Oro, Banco de la República: p. 29
Photolibrary: p. 30
Shutterstock: Pichugin Dmitry: p. 16–17; Herbert Eisengruber:
 p. 12; Front Page: p. 28; Andrzej Gibasiewicz: p. 4–5
 (background); Ramzi Hachicho: p. 22–23 (pyramid image);
 Vladimir Korosty-Shevskiy: p. 5 (foreground); Leksele: p. 8;
 Miaden Mitrinovic: p. 22–23 (geometry equipment);
 Risteskigoce: p. 25; Daniel Wiedemann: p. 14
TopFoto: p. 20; Silvio Fiore: p. 26; Fortean/Aarsleff:
 p. 24; Stapleton/HIP: p. 18
Werner Forman Archive: p. 13

Illustration:
Stefan Chabluk: p. 19

Every effort has been made to trace
the owners of copyrighted material.

Library and Archives Canada Cataloguing in Publication

Walker, Kathryn, 1957-
 Mysteries of the ancients / Kathryn Walker ; based on original
text by Brian Innes.

(Unsolved!)
Includes index.
ISBN 978-0-7787-4147-3 (bound).--ISBN 978-0-7787-4160-2 (pbk.)

 1. Civilization, Ancient--Juvenile literature. 2. Curiosities
and wonders--Juvenile literature. 3. Antiquities--Juvenile literature.
I.°Innes, Brian. Mysteries of the ancients. II. Title. III. Series: Unsolved!
(St. Catharines, Ont.)

CB311.W34 2009   j930   C2009-903113-2

Library of Congress Cataloging-in-Publication Data

Walker, Kathryn.
 Mysteries of the ancients / Kathryn Walker.
 p. cm. -- (Unsolved!)
 Based on: Mysteries of the ancients / Brian Innes. c1999.
 Includes index.
 ISBN 978-0-7787-4160-2 (pbk. : alk. paper)
 -- ISBN 978-0-7787-4147-3 (reinforced library binding : alk. paper)
 1. Civilization, Ancient--Juvenile literature. 2. Curiosities and wonde
Juvenile literature. 3. Antiquities--Juvenile literature. I. Innes, Brian.
Mysteries of the ancients. II. Title.

 CB311.W355 2010
 930--dc22
                                    2009020923

Crabtree Publishing Company

www.crabtreebooks.com   1-800-387-7650

Published in Canada
Crabtree Publishing
616 Welland Ave.
St. Catharines, ON
L2M 5V6

Published in the United States
Crabtree Publishing
PMB16A
350 Fifth Ave., Suite 3308
New York, NY 10118

Published by **CRABTREE PUBLISHING COMPANY in 201**

Contents

Stone Giants

...Mysterious stone statues stand on a remote Pacific island.

On April 5, 1722, three Dutch ships arrived at a small island in the middle of the Pacific Ocean. The island was about 2,200 miles (3,540 km) west of Chile in South America. Jacob Roggeveen was in command of the ships. As it was Easter Sunday, Roggeveen named the place Easter Island.

When he came ashore, Roggeveen saw the most amazing sight. Hundreds of gigantic stone figures stood in rows along the cliffs. The figures had large heads with long, unsmiling faces. Some of them had a red stone hat or crown.

Most of the statues were carved from the stone of a **crater**. The crater was from an **extinct** volcano on the island. There were hundreds of unfinished statues at the crater with carving tools still lying beside them. Why did the work suddenly stop? What did the strange statues mean?

These Easter Island statues stand with their backs to the sea. Hundreds of them stand on platforms around the island. The statues are known as moai.

>> **crater**—The bowl-shaped opening at the top of a volcano

"...Hundreds of gigantic stone figures stood in rows along the cliffs."

How Strange...

Some of the island's stone statues are more than 30 feet (9 m) high.

The statues' ears are long and narrow.

At the time of Jacob Roggeveen's visit, about 4,000 people were living on Easter Island. Many had the yellowy-brown skin and dark hair that is usual for people from the Pacific Islands. But, oddly, others had blue eyes, reddish hair, and light-colored skin.

Slavery!

After news of the island's discovery reached Europe, other people went there. Some of them were **slave traders**. They captured many of the islanders and took them away to be slaves. By the mid-1800s, there were less than 200 natives living on Easter Island.

Visitors to Easter Island in the 1700s are shown here sketching and measuring statues.

Legends of the island

W.J. Thompson was an officer in the U.S. Navy. In the 1880s, he stayed on the island and wrote down legends about its history. Old wooden boards were found that had been carved with a type of picture writing. Sadly, the islanders that Thompson met no longer knew what these signs meant. Perhaps they hold the answers to some of the island's mysteries.

"...slave traders. captured many of the islanders an took them away to be slaves."

>> **slave trader**—A person involved in capturing, selling, and buying people as slave

The natives told Thompson that the first people to settle on the island were Pacific Islanders. They were led by a chief called Hotu-matua. Some stories also told of an older people, the Hanau Eep, or "Long Ears." After Thompson, another visitor was told that the first islanders were very big and had yellow hair. They came from a land that lay "behind America."

Death of the Long Ears

According to one legend, the Long Ears were killed by people called the Hanau-momoko, or "Short Ears." The Short Ears may have been Hotu-matua's people. Only two Long Ears were spared. They became the **ancestors** of the light-skinned islanders. Experts worked out that this killing took place in about 1760.

By 1864, all the statues had been toppled. Some have now been set upright again, but many remain on the ground.

>> **ancestor**—Someone who lived long ago, and from whom a person is descended   **7**

Thor Heyerdahl

In 1955, Norwegian explorer Thor Heyerdahl led a team of scientists to Easter Island. In 1947, Heyerdahl and his team had sailed more than 4,000 miles (6,400 km) across the Pacific Ocean in a wooden raft. By doing this, Heyerdahl proved that early peoples from South America could have sailed across the Pacific in rafts.

Heyerdahl became friends with the **mayor** of Easter Island, a man named Atan. Atan had red hair and claimed to be a Long Ear. He told Heyerdahl that the red crowns on some of the statues represented red hair. He believed that the statues had probably been made in memory of Long Ears who had died.

Heyerdahl thought that the Long Ears might have come from the country of Peru in South America in about 380 A.D. This may be true. But who these red-haired, fair-skinned people were remains a mystery.

Some moai have red crowns or hats. The mayor of the island told Thor Heyerdahl that they were meant to look like red hair.

>> **mayor**—A person elected as head of a local government

Visitors from space?

Swiss writer Erich von Däniken had some unusual ideas about the Easter Island statues. In 1968, his book *Chariots of the Gods?* suggested that **aliens** had visited Earth thousands of years ago. Von Däniken thought the aliens had created huge ancient buildings and statues around the world. Von Däniken said there would not have been enough men on Easter Island to carve the huge statues out of "steel-hard" rock. Also, he said the islanders could not have moved and raised the statues. But the statues are made from rock that is far from steel-hard. Atan had shown Heyerdahl how they could be carved and moved into place. In spite of Thor Heyerdahl's discoveries, some of Easter Island's mysteries remain unsolved. Perhaps, one day, we will learn its true history.

How Strange...

The Toltecs were a people who lived in Mexico more than 1,000 years ago. They raised giant stone statues that are similar in some ways to the moai on Easter Island.

In 1955, Easter Islanders showed Thor Heyerdahl's team how to raise up a moai with poles and rocks.

City in the Clouds

...A great city stands in ruins high in the Andes.

About 45 miles (72 km) from the city of La Paz in Bolivia, South America, there are ancient ruins. They stand high up in the Andes Mountains. Lake Titicaca, which lies across the border between Bolivia and Peru, is 15 miles (24 km) away. These ruins are all that is left of a once magnificent city now known as Tiahuanaco.

One of the first Europeans to see Tiahuanaco was the Spaniard Cieza de León in 1549. At that time, the city had already been in ruins for centuries. De León was told that it had been built by pale-skinned, bearded men who did not look like the natives.

Today, there is even less of Tiahuanaco to see. The remains of only four buildings are left. But it is clear that they once formed a beautiful **ceremonial** center for the Tiahuanacan people.

>> **ceremonial**—Used for ceremonies, such as religious rituals

Many people believe that Tiahuanaco once stood at the edge of Lake Titicaca. Over time, the level of the lake dropped, leaving the city and lake miles (km) apart.

Early visitors did not believe that local people could have built such a big city. Some of them thought giants built it.

*This picture shows ruins of a temple at Tiahuanaco. The city stands high up in the mountains, at more than 2 miles (3.2 km) above **sea level**. For this reason, it is called the "city in the clouds."*

The Akapana

The largest of Tiahuanaco's structures is the Akapana. It is also called the fortress. This is a mound that was covered with stones to create a flat-topped pyramid. The pyramid is about 655 feet (200 m) square at the **base** and 55 feet (17 m) high. A stone stairway led to the top, where experts think there was a large pool.

The Gateway of the Sun, pictured here, has a carved image of the god Viracocha over the doorway.

Gateway of the Sun

The second great stone building is the temple, or Kalasasaya. It has huge stone pillars that may once have supported a roof. Beside the temple stands a 12 foot (3.7 m) high statue of a man. He holds an object that looks like a book.

The most amazing feature of the temple is the Gateway of the Sun. This is made from a single block of stone 10 feet (3 m) long, 11 feet (3.4 m) high, and 3 feet (1 m) thick. A scene is carved into the stone above the doorway. At its center is the figure of a god named Viracocha. Legends say that Viracocha created the world.

"The most amazing feature of the temple is the Gateway of the Sun."

>> **base**—The bottom part of something

he two smaller ruins are known as the
alace and the Gateway of the Puma. Both
ontain huge stone slabs that measure up
37 feet (11 m) long. Some of these slabs
veigh more than 100 tons (90 tonnes).

An earlier view

arly visitors in the 1500s reported seeing
eautiful statues at Tiahuanaco that later
isappeared. They also said that the city
uildings were decorated with gold and
opper ornaments. Stone masks hung
om the walls from big gold nails.

lost of these
easures were
iter stolen, but a
w of them have
een found. The
osnansky Museum in
a Paz has some statues,
ots, and golden figures from
ne city. There are also cups, plates,
poons, and some of the golden nails.

*This **ceramic** jug with a bird's
head was discovered in the
Tiahuanaco area. It was probably
used in religious ceremonies.*

A question of age

Experts disagree about when the city was built. Some say it dates between 300 B.C. and 500 A.D., but others argue that it may date back to 12,000 or even 17,000 B.C.! The earlier dates would make Tiahuanaco the world's oldest city.

In 2000, ruins of a temple and a road were found in Lake Titicaca. Could these have been part of Tiahuanaco? If they were, the city must have existed before the lake was formed. Part of it could have been covered by a great flood.

How was it built?

The stones used to build Tiahuanaco came from an area several miles (km) away. No one knows how the huge stone blocks were moved to the city. Also, the stones were cut with great skill and **precision**. No one knows what tools the workmen used to do this.

"In 2000, ruins of a temple and a road were found in Lake Titicaca."

A man rows o on Lake Titica in a boat made from reeds. Th huge lake cov an area of 3,2 square miles (8,290 square

>> **precision**—Accuracy or exactness

Legend of Tiahuanaco

In the 1500s, Spaniard Juan de Betanzos studied local legends. He was told that in ancient times, the land was in darkness. Then a lord named Kon Tiki Viracocha came from a lake and went to Tiahuanaco. He made the Sun, stars, and Moon. Viracocha also gave rules to men about how they should live.

Similar legends are found throughout South America. All of them describe Viracocha as tall and pale-skinned, with short hair. People built temples **dedicated** to him in many parts of South America.

This picture shows a view of the ruins of Tiahuanaco. Experts believe that as many as 100,000 people may have once lived in the region. No one knows what caused them to leave.

Mysterious city

Sometime between 1000 and 1200, the city of Tiahuanaco was left to fall into ruin. No one is sure why this happened.

Who built Tiahuanaco? Was Viracocha a real man? Until these questions are answered, Tiahuanaco remains a city of mysteries.

>> **dedicated**—Built for the purpose of worshiping, or honoring a god or person

The Great Pyramid

...Egypt's Great Pyramid holds many secrets.

About 10 miles (16 km) southwest of the Egyptian city of Cairo, rises the Great Pyramid of Khufu. Khufu was a pharaoh, or ruler, of ancient Egypt. He is sometimes known by his Greek name, Cheops. The pyramid was completed in about 2560 B.C., making it more than 4,500 years old.

For about 3,800 years, the Great Pyramid was the tallest building on Earth. It stood 479 feet (146 m) high, but its top has since been worn away. It is made up of 2,300,000 stone blocks, each weighing about 2.5 tons (2.3 tonnes). No one is sure how the Egyptians built this pyramid. They might have made a **ramp** around the first blocks, or even inside the structure. Then they could push more blocks up the ramp on rollers.

But what was the Great Pyramid used for? It is likely that it was built as a tomb for the pharaoh. But some people think it had a different purpose.

>> **ramp**—A slope that connects one level to another

This is how the Great Pyramid of Khufu looks today. But when it was newly built, it was covered with white **limestone**.

For about 3,800 years, the Great Pyramid was the tallest building on Earth."

>> **limestone**—A type of rock often used in building

Exploring the pyramid

In about 820 A.D., an Arab leader named Abdullah al Mamun, tried to get inside the Great Pyramid. He gathered a gang of local workmen to help him. Al Mamun had been told there was a secret room inside the pyramid. But he could not find the entrance.

Al Mamum's men stripped away the smooth stone slabs that then covered the outside of the pyramid. They tunneled through the stone blocks underneath. Eventually, the men broke through into a narrow, sloping passage. It led down below the ground. Today, this is known as the **Descending** Passage.

The men explored inside. Eventually, they found the hinged door to the outside of the pyramid. It opened about 50 feet (15 m) above the ground.

Almost 1,200 years ago, al Mamun and his men broke into the Great Pyramid. This painting shows them climbing up into the Grand Gallery.

>> **descending**—Leading from a higher to a lower place

nto the center

l Mamun's team discovered
second passage, now called
he **Ascending** Passage. It
loped up toward the center
f the pyramid. The men found
n opening in the ceiling of
he passage. They climbed up
nto it and found themselves
n a huge, sloping corridor of
mooth stone. This is known
s the Grand Gallery.

The missing pharaoh

The men had reached the center
f the pyramid. They found a large
oom off the Grand Gallery. At one
nd stood a huge stone coffin with
o lid. It was completely empty.

l Mamun had believed he would
nd ancient writings hidden in the
yramid, perhaps even treasure.
nstead, he found nothing. Perhaps
obbers had stolen everything. But
l Mamun said there was no sign of
 break-in. Stone plugs still blocked
he passages to keep out robbers.

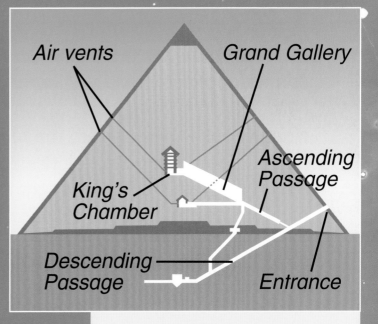

Air vents — *Grand Gallery* — *Ascending Passage* — *King's Chamber* — *Descending Passage* — *Entrance*

This is a plan showing the passages and chambers inside the Great Pyramid. The King's Chamber is where the empty stone coffin stands.

How Strange...

The stone coffin is too
big to fit through any
of the passages. It was
probably put in place
before the pyramid
was completed.

Ancient observatory

In 1798, Frenchman Edmé-François Jomard measured the outside of the pyramid. He determined that the four sides exactly lined up with the four points of the **compass**—north, south, east, and west. Jomard thought the pyramid was built as an observatory. An observatory is where scientists watch and study the planets and stars.

A clue from the past

Eighty years later, Englishman Richard Proctor read a report written by a Roman named Proclus. Proclus lived in the 400s A.D. He said that before it was completed, the Great Pyramid had been used as an observatory.

Proctor was an astronomer—someone who studies the skies. He could see that when the Grand Gallery was still open at the top, astronomers could have used it to watch and measure the positions of the Sun, Moon, planets, and stars. They could have made a map of the sky. It is possible that they might even have worked out the shape and size of Earth.

This picture shows how the Grand Gallery could have been used as an observatory before the Great Pyramid was completed.

>> **compass**—An instrument that shows direction

Hidden secrets

Some people think that when the astronomers had discovered all they wanted to know, they may have walled up their observatory. They did not want anyone else to learn about their methods. This could explain a legend that the pyramid contains the secrets of the universe.

Perhaps the astronomers told the pharaoh he could have the pyramid as his tomb, but did not keep their promise. Or maybe the Great Pyramid was used as Khufu's tomb. There could be rooms inside it that have not been found. One might still contain Khufu's body.

The Grand Gallery inside the Great Pyramid of Khufu, as it is today.

Powers of the Pyramid

..The pyramid still fascinates many people.

During the 19th century, people in Europe became fascinated by ancient Egypt. Some of those who studied the Great Pyramid claimed it had special meanings or amazing powers.

In 1864, astronomer Charles Piazzi Smyth went to Egypt to measure the pyramid. He felt sure that the Egyptians had recorded important facts about Earth and the universe in the pyramid's measurements. For example, Smyth claimed that the length of one side of the pyramid at the base was 365.242 cubits (old units of measure). This is exactly the number of days in a **solar year**.

People have written books about how the measurements of the Great Pyramid and its passages have hidden meanings. Believers in these ideas are known as pyramidologists.

>> **solar year**—The length of time it takes Earth to travel once around the Sun

How Strange...

Some people say that the measurements and shapes of the rooms and passages in the Great Pyramid were a way of recording past events and **predictions** about what was going to happen in the future.

"Some of those who studied the Great Pyramid claimed it had special meanings or amazing powers."

Pyramidologists think that the measurements of the Great Pyramid can reveal all kinds of facts about the universe and even the future.

>> **prediction**—A warning or statement of what will happen in the future

Strange discovery

Frenchman Antoine Bovis visited the Great Pyramid in the 1920s. He saw bodies of cats and other animals that had crept into the King's Chamber and died there. Oddly, the bodies had not rotted. They had mummified, or dried out.

Bovis built a wooden model of a pyramid and put a dead cat inside it. Within a few days, the cat had mummified. Next, he put meat and eggs inside the pyramid. Instead of rotting, they dried out.

Making pyramids

Czech engineer Karel Drbal heard about Bovis's experiments. He made a tiny cardboard pyramid. Drbal claimed that when he put a blunt razor blade inside the pyramid, it became sharp again. In 1959, he began selling Cheops pyramid razor blade sharpeners.

People everywhere started making their own pyramids. Some believed the pyramid shape had healing powers. However, when scientists in California experimented with pyramids, they did not get the same results as Bovis and Drbal.

"People everywhere started making their own pyramids."

Pyramids are used for many purposes. This one in Denmark was built for healing and **meditating**.

>> **meditating**—Thinking about something deeply for a long time

Some people wonder if the Great Pyramid was a signal to visitors from other planets.

Powerful light

When it was first built, the Great Pyramid was covered in gleaming white stone and had a top made of gold. The pyramid would have shone brilliantly in the Egyptian Sun. It would have been visible from many miles away. There are people who believe that the pyramid acted as a signal to alien visitors from space.

The Great Pyramid has fascinated people for centuries. Author William Fix has written books about it. In his book *Pyramid Odyssey*, Fix had this to say about the Great Pyramid: "It is enormous, it is **legendary**... It does not seem to belong to our world."

How Strange...

Some people say that humans living 4,500 years ago did not have the equipment and skills needed to build the Great Pyramid. They think that aliens must have helped build it.

Eldorado

...There are tales of a golden city in the South American jungle.

In the 1500s, Spanish explorers returned to Europe from **expeditions** to South America. They brought with them a wonderful story. They had been told that somewhere, in the heart of South America, stood an ancient city filled with riches.

Every year, the ruler of this city covered his body with gold dust until he looked like a golden statue. Then he sailed out across a lake and plunged into the water, washing the dust away. His people threw gold and jewels into the lake as offerings to the gods.

The Spaniards called the ruler El Dorado, meaning "the **gilded** man." Over time, the word "Eldorado" came to mean a place of fabulous wealth, or somewhere that exists only in the imagination.

How Strange...

Spanish soldier Juan Martinez got lost in the country of Venezuela in 1534. He claimed that natives took him to a city in the jungle called Omagua where he met El Dorado.

>> **expedition**—A trip or journey to find out about something

This is a ceremonial gold mask from Bogotá in Colombia. For centuries, people believed that treasures such as this could be found in the lost city of Eldorado.

The story of Eldorado excited people for many years. There were expeditions to try to find the city. In 1541, Spaniard Francisco de Orellana took part in one of the most famous of these attempts. Orellano became the first person known to sail the length of the Amazon River. But he failed to find the golden city.

More failures

The English explorer Sir Walter Raleigh led two expeditions in search of Eldorado. The first was in 1595 and the second was in 1616. Both of his attempts ended in failure.

In 1925, another English explorer, Colonel Percy H. Fawcett decided to search once more. He had heard about a lost city in southwestern Brazil. Fawcett set off with his son and a friend to find it.

Fawcett sent a message to his wife from the Mato Grosso region of Brazil. He told her he was about to set off into unexplored **territory**. Fawcett and his companions were never seen again.

This picture shows a view over the rainforest in the Mato Grosso region of Brazil. Colonel Fawcett believed that a lost city existed in this area.

>> **territory**—An area of land or a region

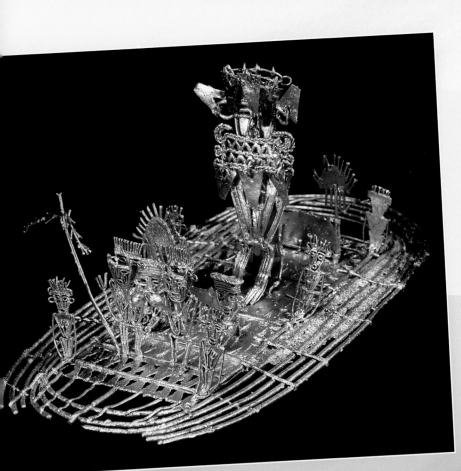

This gold model of El Dorado was found in 1969, close to Lake Guatavita. It is now in a museum in Bogotá.

More clues

Today, people believe that the ceremony of El Dorado took place in Lake Guatavita. This is located about 35 miles (56 km) northeast of Bogotá, capital of Colombia.

In 1969, a beautiful **model** of solid gold was discovered in a cave close to Bogatá. It is a model of a raft. On it stand the figures of El Dorado and his priests. The discovery of the model seems to give truth to legends that link the ceremony to Lake Guatavita.

"The discovery of the model seems to give truth to legends..."

>> **model**—A small copy of something

Greed for gold

Stories about the ceremony of El Dorado told how gold and jewels were thrown into the lake. Greed for these riches attracted many people to Lake Guatavita. For many years, people tried **draining** the lake to find this treasure. However, these attempts were not successful.

Eventually, the government of Colombia made Lake Guatavita a protected area. It forbids any attempt to empty its water or take its treasures.

Lake Guatavita in Colombia is said to be the site of the ancient ceremony of El Dorado.

A lost wonder

There are still no signs of the lost city of gold that Juan Martinez claimed he saw. Large areas of the Mato Grosso region in Brazil remain unexplored. Maybe, one day, a wonderful ruined city will be found there. Or perhaps it must remain forever in stories and in imagination.

"...perhaps [Eldorado] must remain forever in stories and in imagination."

>> **draining**—Emptying of water

Glossary

lien A creature from another planet

ncestor Someone who lived long ago, and from whom a person is descended

scending Leading from a lower to a higher place

ase The bottom part of something

eramic Made from clay or similar material

eremonial Used for ceremonies, such as religious rituals

ompass An instrument that shows direction

ater The bowl-shaped opening at the top of a volcano

edicated Built for the purpose of worshiping, or honoring a god or person

escending Leading from a higher to a lower place

aining Emptying of water

xpedition A trip or journey to find out about something

xtinct No longer active or burning (describing a volcano)

gilded Covered with a layer of gold

legendary Famous because of its greatness

limestone A type of rock often used in building

mayor A person elected as head of a local government

meditating Thinking about something deeply for a long time

model A small copy of something

precision Accuracy or exactness

prediction A warning or statement of what will happen in the future

radar A device that uses radio waves to locate an object

ramp A slope that connects one level to another

sea level The average level of the sea's surface

slave trader A person involved in capturing, selling, and buying people as slaves

solar year The length of time it takes Earth to travel once around the Sun

territory An area of land or a region

Index

Further Reading

• Adams, Simon and Fry, Plantagenet Somerset. *History of the World: Third Edition Revised and Updated.* DK Children, 2007.

• Ash, Russell. *Great Wonders of the World.* DK Children, 2006.

• Kaplan, Sarah Pitt. *The Great Pyramid at Giza: Tomb of Wonders*, "High Interest Books" series. Children's Press, 2005.

• Putnam, James. *Pyramid: DK Eyewitness Books.* DK Children, 2004.

• Underwood, Deborah. *The Easter Island Statues*, "Wonders of the World" series. Kidhaven, 2004.